GPT-5 AND THE US GOVERNMENT
Inside the AI Frontier and Beyond

*Exploring OpenAI's Groundbreaking
Collaboration with the United States and
the Implications for Our Future*

Alejandro S. Diego

Copyright © Alejandro S. Diego, 2024.

All rights reserved. No part of this publication may be reproduced, distributed, or transmitted in any form or by any means, including photocopying, recording, or other electronic or mechanical methods, without the prior written permission of the publisher, except in the case of brief quotations embodied in critical reviews and certain other noncommercial uses permitted by copyright law.

Table of Contents

Introduction..4
Chapter 1: The Rise of GPT-5......................8
Chapter 2: Strategic Partnership with the US Government.. 19
Chapter 3: Addressing AI Safety Concerns.............28
Chapter 4: Ethical and Societal Considerations......38
Chapter 5: Privacy and Government Oversight.......44
Chapter 6: Future of AI Governance........................55
Conclusion..61

Introduction

The announcement of OpenAI's collaboration with the US government on the development of GPT-5 sent shockwaves through the tech world and beyond. In an era where artificial intelligence is reshaping industries, transforming everyday life, and pushing the boundaries of what we thought possible, this groundbreaking partnership marks a new frontier in AI innovation and governance.

Imagine a world where AI models not only understand but anticipate human needs with unprecedented accuracy. GPT-5 promises to be more than just a tool; it is poised to become an integral part of our daily lives, influencing everything from healthcare and education to creative arts and scientific research. OpenAI's bold decision to grant the US government early access to this advanced AI model is not just a technological leap but a strategic move with profound implications.

The significance of this move cannot be overstated. OpenAI, already a leader in AI development, has chosen to prioritize safety and ethical considerations by partnering with the US AI Safety Institute. This institute, established under the National Institute of Standards and Technology (NIST), will play a crucial role in developing guidelines and policies for AI measurement and safety. By involving a federal body at this stage, OpenAI is sending a clear message: the future of AI must be built on a foundation of responsibility and rigorous oversight.

But why now? The timing of this collaboration is particularly intriguing. Earlier this year, OpenAI disbanded its super alignment team, a group dedicated to ensuring AI systems align with human intentions. This decision led to the departure of key figures and raised concerns within the AI community about the company's direction. Critics questioned whether OpenAI was prioritizing rapid development over safety. The partnership with the US government can be seen as a direct response to these criticisms, an assurance that safety remains a top priority.

The objectives of this partnership are multifaceted. First and foremost, it aims to advance the science of AI evaluations. By working with the US AI Safety Institute, OpenAI hopes to develop robust evaluation methods that can be applied to future AI models. This collaboration is also about setting a precedent for AI governance. As AI systems become more integrated into critical infrastructure and decision-making processes, the need for clear and effective governance becomes paramount.

In this book, we will delve into the intricacies of this collaboration, exploring its potential impact on the future of AI and society. We will examine the capabilities of GPT-5, the safety measures being put in place, and the ethical considerations that come with such powerful technology. Through this journey, we aim to provide a comprehensive understanding of how OpenAI's bold move is shaping the AI landscape and what it means for all of us.

Prepare to embark on a journey into the heart of AI innovation, where technology meets governance, and the future unfolds before our eyes. The story of GPT-5 and its collaboration with the US government is not just about a new AI model; it's about the dawn of a new era in artificial intelligence. This is a tale of ambition, responsibility, and the relentless pursuit of progress. Welcome to the AI frontier and beyond.

Chapter 1: The Rise of GPT-5

OpenAI's journey in the development of AI models has been nothing short of remarkable. The evolution from GPT-1 to GPT-4 has showcased a series of groundbreaking advancements that have pushed the boundaries of what artificial intelligence can achieve. This progression not only highlights the technical prowess of OpenAI but also underscores the growing impact of these models on various aspects of society.

The story begins with GPT-1, the first iteration in the Generative Pre-trained Transformer series. Launched in 2018, GPT-1 was a significant step forward in the field of natural language processing (NLP). It introduced the concept of pre-training on a large corpus of text data, followed by fine-tuning for specific tasks. This approach allowed GPT-1 to generate coherent and contextually relevant text, albeit with some limitations in complexity and understanding. Despite its nascent capabilities, GPT-1 laid the groundwork for future iterations, demonstrating the potential of large-scale language models.

Building on this foundation, OpenAI introduced GPT-2 in 2019. GPT-2 represented a substantial leap in performance and capabilities. With 1.5 billion parameters, it was more than ten times larger than GPT-1, enabling it to generate more sophisticated and contextually aware responses. The release of GPT-2 also sparked widespread attention and debate due to its ability to produce highly convincing and human-like text. Concerns about misuse and ethical implications led OpenAI to initially withhold the full model, a decision that underscored the need for careful consideration of AI's potential risks.

In 2020, OpenAI unveiled GPT-3, a model that truly captured the imagination of the world. Boasting an astonishing 175 billion parameters, GPT-3 set a new benchmark for AI capabilities. It demonstrated an unprecedented ability to understand and generate human-like text across a wide range of tasks, from writing essays and composing poetry to answering complex questions and generating programming code. GPT-3's versatility and depth of understanding were game-changing, opening up new possibilities for applications in education, business, healthcare, and beyond. Its success also highlighted the challenges of managing such powerful technology, including issues related to bias, fairness, and ethical use.

Throughout these iterations, OpenAI achieved numerous breakthroughs and milestones. One of the key innovations was the development of the transformer architecture, which enabled the models to process and generate text more efficiently and accurately than previous approaches. Additionally, the concept of transfer learning—pre-training on vast amounts of data followed by fine-tuning—proved to be highly effective in enhancing the models' performance across diverse tasks.

The evolution from GPT-1 to GPT-3 was marked by a relentless pursuit of scaling up both the size of the models and the datasets used for training. This scaling played a crucial role in enhancing the models' ability to generate contextually rich and coherent text. It also brought to the forefront the importance of responsible AI development, as the potential for misuse and unintended consequences grew alongside the models' capabilities.

With each iteration, OpenAI not only pushed the technical boundaries of AI but also grappled with the broader implications of its creations. The journey from GPT-1 to GPT-3 set the stage for GPT-4, which continued this trajectory of innovation and responsibility. GPT-4, while less publicized than its predecessor, built upon the strengths of GPT-3 and addressed some of its limitations, further refining the model's understanding and generation of human language.

As we stand on the cusp of the next leap forward with GPT-5, it's essential to reflect on the journey that brought us here. The evolution of OpenAI's AI models is a testament to the power of innovation, the importance of ethical considerations, and the transformative potential of artificial intelligence. The breakthroughs and milestones achieved along the way have not only advanced the field of AI but have also set the stage for a future where AI can play a more integrated and beneficial role in our lives.

As we anticipate the release of GPT-5, the expectations surrounding its capabilities are monumental. Building on the strengths and lessons of its predecessors, GPT-5 promises to introduce innovations and advancements that could redefine the landscape of artificial intelligence. The journey from GPT-1 to GPT-4 has set a high bar, but GPT-5 is poised to surpass it, bringing new levels of sophistication and utility to AI technology.

One of the most eagerly anticipated advancements in GPT-5 is its ability to understand and generate human language with even greater nuance and accuracy. With a larger and more refined parameter set, GPT-5 is expected to handle context, ambiguity, and complex language structures more effectively than ever before. This improvement will likely enhance its performance across a wide range of applications, from natural language processing and translation to content generation and interactive dialogue systems.

In addition to language capabilities, GPT-5 is expected to bring significant innovations in areas such as multi-modal learning and integration. This means the model could seamlessly process and generate content that combines text, images, audio, and possibly even video, opening up new possibilities for creative and interactive applications. Imagine an AI that can not only write an article but also create accompanying visuals and provide a synthesized voice-over, all tailored to specific user preferences and context.

The potential impact of GPT-5 on various sectors is vast. In healthcare, for example, it could assist in diagnosing diseases by analyzing patient data and medical literature, providing doctors with more accurate and comprehensive insights. In education, GPT-5 could revolutionize personalized learning by offering tailored tutoring and educational content that adapts to individual student needs and learning styles. The business sector could see significant benefits as well, with AI-driven insights improving decision-making, customer service, and operational efficiency.

The creative industries stand to gain tremendously from GPT-5's advancements. Writers, artists, and musicians could leverage its capabilities to generate new ideas, streamline workflows, and enhance their creative processes. In entertainment, GPT-5 could be used to create more immersive and interactive experiences, from video games to virtual reality environments. The potential applications are limited only by our imagination and ability to harness this powerful technology responsibly.

The reactions and speculations surrounding GPT-5 have been intense. The tech community is abuzz with discussions about its potential capabilities and the implications of its release. Many experts believe that GPT-5 will set a new standard for AI models, pushing the boundaries of what is possible in natural language understanding and generation. There is also considerable excitement about its potential to integrate more seamlessly with other technologies, creating more holistic and versatile AI systems.

However, with great power comes great responsibility. Industry experts have expressed both excitement and caution regarding GPT-5. While its potential benefits are immense, there are also significant concerns about the ethical and societal implications of such a powerful AI. Issues such as data privacy, AI bias, and the potential for misuse are at the forefront of these discussions. The need for robust safety measures and ethical guidelines is more critical than ever, and OpenAI's collaboration with the US government is seen as a step in the right direction.

The tech community's response has been a mix of anticipation and critical scrutiny. Many are eager to see how GPT-5 will perform in real-world applications and what new possibilities it will unlock. There is also significant interest in the safety and governance frameworks that will be implemented to manage its deployment. The broader AI research community is watching closely, as the lessons learned from GPT-5 will likely inform future AI development and policy decisions.

Industry experts' predictions about GPT-5's impact vary, but there is a consensus that it will be a transformative force in the AI landscape. Some predict that it will accelerate the adoption of AI across industries, leading to new efficiencies and capabilities. Others caution that the societal implications of such advanced AI must be carefully managed to avoid potential pitfalls and ensure that the benefits are broadly shared.

In summary, the expected capabilities of GPT-5 are poised to push the boundaries of artificial intelligence to new heights. Its innovations and advancements could have far-reaching impacts on numerous sectors, transforming the way we interact with technology and each other. The reactions and speculations from the tech community and industry experts underscore the significance of this development, highlighting both the opportunities and challenges that lie ahead. As we stand on the brink of this new era, the story of GPT-5 is one of ambition, innovation, and the quest for responsible AI advancement.

Chapter 2: Strategic Partnership with the US Government

The collaboration between OpenAI and the US government regarding GPT-5 was formally announced by Sam Altman, CEO of OpenAI, on the social media platform X. This partnership marks a significant step in the development and governance of artificial intelligence, underscoring the importance of safety and ethical considerations as AI technologies become increasingly advanced and integrated into various aspects of society.

Sam Altman's announcement highlighted the key elements and objectives of this partnership. He emphasized that OpenAI's decision to collaborate with the US AI Safety Institute was driven by a commitment to ensuring that the development of GPT-5 prioritizes safety and ethical considerations. By involving a federal body in the early stages of GPT-5's development, OpenAI aims to address growing concerns about the potential risks and implications of powerful AI systems.

The US AI Safety Institute, established under the National Institute of Standards and Technology (NIST), plays a crucial role in this collaboration. The Institute's primary mission is to develop guidelines and policies for AI measurement and safety, ensuring that AI systems are evaluated rigorously and systematically. By partnering with the US AI Safety Institute, OpenAI seeks to leverage the Institute's expertise and resources to create a robust framework for the evaluation and governance of GPT-5.

The partnership is designed to achieve several key objectives. First and foremost, it aims to advance the science of AI evaluations by developing new methods and standards for assessing the safety and performance of AI models. This involves not only technical evaluations but also ethical and societal considerations, ensuring that the deployment of AI technologies aligns with broader public interests and values.

Another critical aspect of the collaboration is the emphasis on transparency and accountability. OpenAI and the US AI Safety Institute are committed to maintaining open lines of communication with the public and the broader AI research community. This includes sharing information about the development and evaluation processes, as well as the results of safety assessments. By fostering a culture of transparency, the partnership aims to build trust and confidence in the responsible development and use of AI technologies.

The role of the US AI Safety Institute in this partnership cannot be overstated. As a federal body with a mandate to ensure the safe and ethical use of AI, the Institute brings a level of oversight and accountability that is crucial for managing the potential risks associated with advanced AI systems. The Institute's involvement provides a formal mechanism for addressing concerns about AI safety and governance, helping to ensure that the development of GPT-5 is conducted in a manner that prioritizes public safety and ethical standards.

This collaboration is also notable for its potential to set precedents in the field of AI governance. By involving a federal body in the development of a cutting-edge AI model, OpenAI and the US AI Safety Institute are establishing a model for how public and private sectors can work together to address the challenges and opportunities presented by advanced AI technologies. This partnership could serve as a blueprint for future collaborations, helping to shape the development and governance of AI on a global scale.

In summary, the partnership between OpenAI and the US government, announced by Sam Altman, represents a bold and proactive approach to the development of GPT-5. By involving the US AI Safety Institute, OpenAI is taking significant steps to ensure that the development of this powerful AI model is conducted with the highest standards of safety and ethical consideration. This collaboration not only aims to advance the science of AI evaluations but also sets a precedent for future partnerships between public and private sectors in the field of AI governance.

The partnership between OpenAI and the US government through the US AI Safety Institute is driven by several critical objectives, with safety and ethical considerations at the forefront. As artificial intelligence continues to evolve and become more integrated into daily life, the potential for both positive impact and unintended consequences grows. This collaboration aims to navigate these complexities, ensuring that the development and deployment of GPT-5 are aligned with the highest standards of safety and ethics.

The primary objective of the partnership is to enhance the safety protocols and ethical frameworks surrounding the development of GPT-5. With the increasing power and sophistication of AI models, ensuring their safe and responsible use is paramount. This involves rigorous testing and evaluation to identify and mitigate potential risks, such as biases in AI decision-making, vulnerabilities to manipulation, and the ethical implications of deploying such advanced technology in various sectors. The partnership seeks to establish comprehensive guidelines that govern the ethical use of GPT-5, ensuring that its deployment benefits society while minimizing harm.

Another key objective is to advance the science of AI evaluations. The US AI Safety Institute is tasked with developing new methods and standards for assessing AI models' safety, performance, and ethical implications. This involves creating robust evaluation frameworks that can be applied not only to GPT-5 but to future AI models as well. These frameworks will help ensure that AI systems are thoroughly tested for safety and ethical compliance before they are deployed in real-world applications.

The goals of the US AI Safety Institute in this partnership are multifaceted. The Institute aims to set the benchmark for AI safety standards, providing a model for other countries and organizations to follow. By establishing clear and effective guidelines, the Institute seeks to foster an environment of trust and accountability in AI development. This includes promoting transparency in the AI development process, encouraging open dialogue between developers, regulators, and the public, and ensuring that AI technologies are developed with public interest in mind.

Historically, AI collaborations with governments have played a crucial role in shaping the development and governance of artificial intelligence. These partnerships have helped establish the necessary regulatory frameworks and safety standards to manage the rapid advancement of AI technologies. One notable example is OpenAI's previous collaboration with the UK government. This partnership involved sharing AI models and research with the UK government to inform policy decisions and regulatory frameworks. The collaboration aimed to address similar concerns about AI safety and ethical use, providing valuable insights into how public and private sectors can work together to govern AI development.

Comparing OpenAI's collaboration with the UK government to the current partnership with the US government highlights several similarities and differences. Both collaborations emphasize the importance of safety and ethical considerations in AI development. They involve close cooperation between AI developers and government bodies to establish robust evaluation and governance frameworks. However, the partnership with the US government is particularly noteworthy due to the scale and potential impact of GPT-5. This collaboration involves a more formalized approach through the US AI Safety Institute, which brings a higher level of oversight and accountability. Additionally, the involvement of a federal body like NIST underscores the commitment to integrating AI safety and ethical considerations into national standards and policies.

In summary, the objectives of the partnership between OpenAI and the US government center around enhancing safety and ethical standards in AI development. The US AI Safety Institute plays a pivotal role in achieving these goals, advancing the science of AI evaluations, and setting benchmarks for global AI safety standards. The historical context of AI collaborations with governments provides valuable insights into the importance of such partnerships, with the current collaboration marking a significant step forward in ensuring the responsible development and deployment of advanced AI technologies like GPT-5.

Chapter 3: Addressing AI Safety Concerns

OpenAI has undergone significant internal changes as it navigates the complex landscape of artificial intelligence development. One of the most notable changes was the disbanding of its super alignment team. This team was initially formed to ensure that AI systems developed by OpenAI aligned with human intentions and ethical standards. The decision to disband this team raised eyebrows within the AI community, sparking concerns about the company's commitment to safety and ethical considerations.

The departure of key figures like Yan Ley and Ilia Sutskever further amplified these concerns. Both were instrumental in advancing OpenAI's research and development, and their exits were seen as indicative of potential internal discord regarding the company's direction and priorities. Yan Ley and

Ilia Sutskever were not just leading researchers; they were also vocal advocates for ensuring that AI technologies were developed responsibly. Their departures were met with a mixture of surprise and apprehension, as many wondered how OpenAI would continue to prioritize safety and ethics without their leadership.

Despite these significant changes, OpenAI has reiterated its commitment to safety. CEO Sam Altman has publicly stated that the company remains dedicated to ensuring that its AI models are developed and deployed responsibly. One of the key measures OpenAI has taken is the allocation of a substantial portion of its computing resources to safety projects. Altman has emphasized that at least 20% of OpenAI's computing power is dedicated to research and initiatives aimed at enhancing AI safety and mitigating potential risks.

Public statements by Sam Altman have sought to reassure both the public and the AI community that safety remains a top priority for OpenAI. He has consistently highlighted the importance of rigorous safety evaluations and ethical considerations in the development of AI technologies. Altman's communication underscores a proactive approach to addressing the potential risks associated with advanced AI systems. By openly discussing the challenges and the measures OpenAI is taking to address them, Altman aims to foster transparency and build trust.

These internal changes and the company's continued commitment to safety are crucial in the context of its partnership with the US government on GPT-5. The collaboration with the US AI Safety Institute is a clear indication that OpenAI is seeking external oversight and expertise to ensure that its AI models are evaluated and governed appropriately. This partnership also serves to counteract any perceptions that the internal changes at OpenAI might have compromised its dedication to safety and ethical considerations.

The allocation of computing resources to safety projects is particularly significant. It demonstrates that OpenAI is not merely paying lip service to the importance of safety but is actively investing in the necessary infrastructure and research to support this commitment. This includes developing new methods for evaluating AI models, identifying potential biases, and ensuring that the models align with ethical standards.

In his public statements, Sam Altman has also addressed the broader implications of AI development. He acknowledges that the rapid advancement of AI technologies brings both tremendous opportunities and significant risks. By prioritizing safety and ethical considerations, OpenAI aims to navigate this dual-edged sword carefully, maximizing the benefits of AI while minimizing its potential harms.

In summary, the internal changes at OpenAI, including the disbanding of the super alignment team and the departure of key figures, have raised important questions about the company's direction. However, OpenAI's continued commitment to safety, as evidenced by the allocation of resources and public statements by Sam Altman, underscores its dedication to developing AI responsibly. The collaboration with the US government further reinforces this commitment, positioning OpenAI at the forefront of safe and ethical AI development.

The US AI Safety Institute plays a pivotal role in the collaboration between OpenAI and the US government, particularly concerning the development of GPT-5. This institute, established under the National Institute of Standards and Technology (NIST), is tasked with developing comprehensive guidelines and policies to ensure the safe and ethical deployment of AI technologies. The involvement of the US AI Safety Institute is crucial in setting the benchmark for AI safety and governance, ensuring that advanced AI models like GPT-5 are developed with the highest standards of oversight and accountability.

One of the primary responsibilities of the US AI Safety Institute is to create robust guidelines for AI measurement and policy. These guidelines are designed to address a wide range of issues, including the technical performance of AI models, their ethical implications, and their potential societal impact. By establishing clear and stringent standards, the Institute aims to ensure that AI systems are thoroughly evaluated before they are deployed. This includes assessing the accuracy, reliability, and fairness of AI models, as well as identifying and mitigating any biases or vulnerabilities they may possess.

The guidelines developed by the US AI Safety Institute serve as a framework for both the development and deployment of AI technologies. They provide a structured approach to evaluating AI models, ensuring that all relevant factors are considered. This holistic approach helps to prevent potential negative outcomes and ensures that AI systems are aligned with societal values and ethical standards. The guidelines also promote transparency and accountability, requiring developers to document their processes and make their findings available for public scrutiny.

The integration of safety initiatives into GPT-5's development is another critical aspect of the US AI Safety Institute's role. This involves embedding safety protocols and ethical considerations into every stage of the AI development process. From the initial design and training of the model to its deployment and ongoing monitoring, safety initiatives are woven into the fabric of GPT-5's development.

During the design phase, the US AI Safety Institute collaborates with OpenAI to ensure that safety and ethical considerations are prioritized. This includes selecting diverse and representative training data to minimize biases and developing algorithms that can detect and correct any issues that arise. The Institute also oversees the creation of mechanisms that allow the AI model to explain its decisions and actions, enhancing transparency and accountability.

In the training phase, the US AI Safety Institute works with OpenAI to implement rigorous testing and evaluation procedures. This involves subjecting GPT-5 to a variety of scenarios and challenges to assess its performance and identify any potential risks. The Institute's guidelines ensure that these evaluations are comprehensive and include assessments of the model's ability to handle ambiguous or unexpected inputs, its robustness against manipulation, and its adherence to ethical standards.

Once GPT-5 is deployed, the US AI Safety Institute continues to play an oversight role, monitoring the model's performance and addressing any issues that arise. This includes ongoing assessments to ensure that the model remains accurate, reliable, and fair. The Institute also works with OpenAI to develop mechanisms for reporting and addressing any unintended consequences or ethical concerns that emerge during the model's use.

The US AI Safety Institute's role in integrating safety initiatives into GPT-5's development highlights the importance of a proactive and comprehensive approach to AI governance. By embedding safety and ethical considerations into every stage of the development process, the Institute helps to ensure that GPT-5 is not only a powerful and innovative AI model but also a responsible and trustworthy one. This approach sets a new standard for AI development, demonstrating how public and private sectors can collaborate to address the challenges and opportunities presented by advanced AI technologies.

In summary, the US AI Safety Institute is instrumental in shaping the development and deployment of GPT-5 through its guidelines for AI measurement and policy and the integration of safety initiatives. Its comprehensive and proactive approach ensures that GPT-5 is developed with the highest standards of safety and ethics, setting a precedent for future AI governance and collaboration between public and private sectors.

Chapter 4: Ethical and Societal Considerations

The anticipated release of GPT-5 by OpenAI is set to make waves across multiple industries, promising advancements that could significantly enhance productivity, innovation, and user experience. However, these benefits come with concerns about job displacement and the potential homogenization of creative output. Thus, the need for robust ethical guidelines and safeguards to prevent misuse is paramount.

In the healthcare industry, GPT-5's advanced natural language processing capabilities can revolutionize patient care and medical research. Imagine AI-driven systems that can swiftly analyze vast amounts of medical data, providing doctors with precise diagnoses and personalized treatment plans. GPT-5 could assist in interpreting complex medical literature, helping researchers stay abreast of the latest developments and facilitating groundbreaking discoveries. Additionally, its ability to handle patient inquiries and provide detailed explanations of medical conditions and treatments can enhance patient engagement and satisfaction.

Education stands to benefit enormously from GPT-5's capabilities. Personalized learning experiences can be created by leveraging its ability to understand and adapt to individual learning styles and needs. Teachers can use GPT-5 to generate customized lesson plans, provide instant feedback on assignments, and offer additional resources tailored to each student's progress. Moreover, GPT-5 can serve as an invaluable tool for language learning, offering real-time translation and conversational practice. Its capacity to generate high-quality educational content can also support curriculum development, ensuring that learning materials are always up-to-date and relevant.

The finance sector can harness GPT-5's analytical power to improve decision-making processes and customer service. Financial institutions can utilize GPT-5 to analyze market trends, predict economic shifts, and generate insightful reports. Customer service chatbots powered by GPT-5 can handle complex inquiries, offer financial advice, and assist with transactions, all while providing a seamless user experience. Furthermore, its ability to detect patterns and anomalies can enhance fraud detection and risk management, ensuring the security and stability of financial systems.

In the creative industries, GPT-5 offers exciting possibilities for content creation and innovation. Writers, artists, and musicians can use GPT-5 to generate new ideas, draft scripts, compose music, and create visual art. Its ability to understand and mimic different styles can help creators experiment with new techniques and expand their artistic horizons. However, this potential comes with concerns about the homogenization of creative output, as the widespread use of AI-generated content could lead to a loss of originality and diversity in the arts.

One of the most significant concerns related to the deployment of GPT-5 is the potential for job displacement. As AI systems become more capable, there is a risk that certain jobs, particularly those involving repetitive or data-driven tasks, may be automated. This shift could lead to economic disruption and exacerbate existing inequalities. It is essential to address these concerns by developing strategies to support workers affected by automation, such as reskilling programs and policies that promote job creation in emerging fields.

The potential homogenization of creative output is another critical issue. While GPT-5 can generate impressive and diverse content, there is a risk that reliance on AI-generated material could stifle human creativity and lead to a more uniform cultural landscape. Ensuring that AI serves as a tool to enhance rather than replace human creativity will be vital in preserving the richness and diversity of artistic expression.

Given these challenges, the need for robust ethical guidelines and safeguards is clear. Ethical guidelines must be established to govern the development and use of GPT-5, ensuring that it aligns with societal values and promotes the common good. These guidelines should address issues such as fairness, transparency, accountability, and privacy. They should also ensure that AI systems are designed to minimize biases and prevent discrimination.

Safeguards are necessary to prevent the misuse of GPT-5. This includes implementing robust security measures to protect against malicious use, such as generating disinformation or conducting cyberattacks. It also involves creating mechanisms for monitoring and addressing unintended consequences, ensuring that any negative impacts are swiftly identified and mitigated. Engaging stakeholders from various sectors, including government, industry, academia, and civil society, will be crucial in developing and enforcing these guidelines and safeguards.

In conclusion, GPT-5 has the potential to significantly impact various industries, offering advancements that can transform healthcare, education, finance, and the creative arts. However, these benefits must be balanced with concerns about job displacement and the homogenization of creative output. Developing robust ethical guidelines and safeguards will be essential in ensuring that GPT-5 is used responsibly and equitably, maximizing its benefits while minimizing its risks. As we stand on the brink of this new era in AI, it is our collective responsibility to navigate these challenges thoughtfully and proactively, ensuring that the future of AI serves the interests of all humanity.

Chapter 5: Privacy and Government Oversight

The collaboration between OpenAI and the US government in developing GPT-5 brings with it significant concerns about data privacy. As AI systems become more advanced and integrated into various aspects of daily life, the need to protect user data and ensure transparency and accountability in their deployment becomes increasingly critical.

One of the primary data privacy concerns revolves around federal access to GPT-5's inner workings. The partnership with the US AI Safety Institute means that federal authorities will have some level of access to the development and evaluation processes of GPT-5. While this is essential for ensuring the AI's safety and compliance with ethical standards, it raises questions about the extent of this access and how user data will be protected. There is a need to strike a balance between allowing sufficient oversight to ensure safety and maintaining the confidentiality and privacy of user data.

To address these concerns, robust safeguards for user data must be implemented. This includes encrypting data at rest and in transit, ensuring that only authorized personnel have access to sensitive information, and employing rigorous access controls to prevent unauthorized use. Additionally, anonymizing data wherever possible can help protect user privacy while still allowing for the necessary oversight and evaluation processes. OpenAI and the US AI Safety Institute must work together to establish these safeguards, ensuring that user data is handled with the utmost care and respect.

Transparency and accountability are crucial in maintaining public trust in the development and deployment of AI technologies like GPT-5. Measures for ensuring transparency should include open communication about the objectives, processes, and outcomes of the partnership. This involves regularly publishing reports on the progress of GPT-5's development, including details on the safety evaluations and ethical considerations that are being addressed. By providing the public with clear and comprehensive information, OpenAI and the US AI Safety Institute can demonstrate their commitment to responsible AI development.

Accountability mechanisms are also essential to ensure that any potential issues are promptly identified and addressed. One such mechanism is the establishment of an independent oversight committee comprised of experts from various fields, including AI ethics, data privacy, and cybersecurity. This committee would be responsible for reviewing the development and deployment processes of GPT-5, ensuring that they comply with established guidelines and standards. Additionally, this committee could serve as an intermediary between the public and the developers, providing a platform for concerns and feedback to be raised and addressed.

Another accountability mechanism involves creating clear protocols for handling data breaches or misuse. This includes establishing a rapid response team to investigate and mitigate any incidents, as well as setting up channels for users to report potential issues. By having these protocols in place, OpenAI and the US AI Safety Institute can demonstrate their commitment to protecting user data and maintaining the integrity of the AI development process.

Furthermore, it is essential to foster a culture of accountability within the organizations involved. This can be achieved by providing regular training on data privacy and ethical considerations for all employees, ensuring that everyone involved in the development and deployment of GPT-5 understands the importance of these issues and their role in addressing them. Encouraging a sense of responsibility and ethical awareness among the workforce can help prevent potential issues and promote a more conscientious approach to AI development.

In summary, the collaboration between OpenAI and the US government on GPT-5 brings significant data privacy concerns that must be addressed through robust safeguards, transparency measures, and accountability mechanisms. Ensuring the protection of user data while allowing for necessary oversight is a delicate balance that requires careful consideration and proactive measures. By implementing comprehensive data privacy safeguards, maintaining transparency through open communication, and establishing strong accountability mechanisms, OpenAI and the US AI Safety Institute can work together to build public trust and ensure the responsible development and deployment of GPT-5. This approach will help to maximize the benefits of this powerful AI technology while minimizing its potential risks, paving the way for a future where AI serves the interests of all humanity.

The collaboration between OpenAI and the US government on GPT-5 is likely to have profound global implications, influencing the trajectory of AI development worldwide. This partnership, which emphasizes safety and ethical considerations, sets a new standard for how advanced AI models should be developed and governed. As countries around the world observe and respond to this collaboration, several key impacts on global AI development and the potential emergence of AI nationalism can be anticipated.

One of the primary global implications of this partnership is its influence on international standards for AI safety and ethics. By partnering with the US AI Safety Institute, OpenAI is demonstrating a commitment to rigorous evaluation and oversight. This move could encourage other countries to adopt similar standards, fostering a more consistent and cohesive approach to AI governance worldwide. International organizations, such as the United Nations and the European Union, may look to this partnership as a model for developing their own AI policies and frameworks, promoting global cooperation and harmonization in AI regulation.

Additionally, the collaboration is likely to accelerate the pace of AI development globally. As GPT-5 sets new benchmarks for AI capabilities, other countries and AI developers will be motivated to push the boundaries of their own research and development efforts. This competitive drive can lead to rapid advancements in AI technology, benefiting various sectors such as healthcare, education, finance, and creative industries. However, this also underscores the need for robust safety and ethical guidelines to ensure that these advancements are used responsibly and do not exacerbate existing inequalities or create new risks.

The partnership between OpenAI and the US government also highlights the growing strategic importance of AI in geopolitics. As AI technologies become more integrated into national security, economic development, and critical infrastructure, countries may begin to view AI capabilities as a key element of their national power. This could lead to the emergence of an era of AI nationalism, where nations prioritize the development and deployment of their own AI technologies to secure a competitive advantage on the global stage.

AI nationalism could manifest in several ways. Countries might invest heavily in domestic AI research and development, aiming to create homegrown AI models that rival those of international competitors. This could lead to increased funding for AI education and innovation, as well as the establishment of national AI research institutes and centers of excellence. Governments may also implement policies to protect and promote their domestic AI industries, such as providing subsidies, tax incentives, or regulatory support.

At the same time, AI nationalism could result in a more fragmented global AI landscape. As countries focus on developing their own AI technologies, there may be less collaboration and knowledge sharing across borders. This could hinder the collective progress of the global AI community, as researchers and developers become more insular and less willing to share their findings and innovations. Additionally, competition between nations could lead to a race to deploy AI technologies without fully considering the long-term implications and risks, potentially resulting in ethical lapses and unintended consequences.

The potential for AI nationalism also raises concerns about the weaponization of AI technologies. As countries strive to maintain a strategic edge, there may be increased investment in AI applications for military and defense purposes. This could include the development of autonomous weapons systems, AI-driven cyber capabilities, and surveillance technologies. The militarization of AI presents significant ethical and security challenges, as the use of AI in warfare and national security contexts could lead to unforeseen consequences and escalate global tensions.

To mitigate the risks associated with AI nationalism, it is essential to foster international cooperation and dialogue on AI governance. Multilateral forums and agreements can play a crucial role in establishing common principles and standards for AI development, ensuring that safety, ethics, and human rights are prioritized. By promoting transparency, accountability, and mutual understanding, the international community can work together to address the challenges posed by advanced AI technologies and harness their potential for the common good.

In conclusion, the collaboration between OpenAI and the US government on GPT-5 is likely to have significant global implications, influencing AI development and governance worldwide. While this partnership sets a positive example for safety and ethical considerations, it also highlights the potential for AI nationalism and the strategic importance of AI in geopolitics. To ensure that the benefits of AI are maximized and its risks minimized, it is crucial to foster international cooperation and establish robust global standards for AI development and deployment. By working together, the global community can navigate the complexities of the AI frontier and build a future where AI technologies serve the interests of all humanity.

Chapter 6: Future of AI Governance

The collaboration between OpenAI and the US government on GPT-5 is setting a critical precedent for the future of AI development and governance. This partnership underscores the importance of safety, ethical considerations, and robust regulatory frameworks in the development of advanced AI technologies. By demonstrating a commitment to these principles, OpenAI and the US government are paving the way for future AI governance that prioritizes public interest and ethical standards.

The significance of this collaboration lies in its potential to influence future AI governance models globally. As AI technologies become more powerful and pervasive, the need for comprehensive and effective governance structures becomes increasingly urgent. The partnership between OpenAI and the US AI Safety Institute serves as a model for how public and private sectors can work together to address the complexities of AI development. This collaboration highlights the importance of integrating safety and ethical considerations into every stage of AI development, from initial design to deployment and monitoring.

One of the key ways this collaboration is setting a precedent is by emphasizing the role of private companies in shaping public policy. Historically, technological advancements have often outpaced regulatory frameworks, leading to challenges in governance and oversight. However, this partnership illustrates how private companies, like OpenAI, can take proactive steps to engage with regulatory bodies and contribute to the development of policies that ensure the safe and ethical use of AI technologies. By actively participating in the creation of guidelines and standards, private companies can help shape public policy in a way that aligns with societal values and promotes the common good.

The implications for government policy are significant. This collaboration demonstrates the potential for governments to work closely with leading AI developers to establish comprehensive regulatory frameworks that address the unique challenges posed by advanced AI systems. By involving the US AI Safety Institute, the government is taking a proactive approach to AI governance, ensuring that safety and ethical considerations are integral to the development process. This approach can serve as a blueprint for other governments looking to develop their own AI policies, fostering a more consistent and cohesive global regulatory environment.

The importance of a collaborative approach between AI developers and regulatory bodies cannot be overstated. Effective governance of AI technologies requires a deep understanding of both the technical and ethical dimensions of AI systems. By collaborating with regulatory bodies, AI developers can ensure that their technologies are evaluated rigorously and meet the highest standards of safety and ethics. This collaboration also helps to build trust between the public, private sectors, and the broader community, demonstrating a shared commitment to responsible AI development.

The potential benefits of a collaborative approach are numerous. Firstly, it promotes transparency and accountability in AI development. By working together, AI developers and regulatory bodies can create mechanisms for regular reporting and public disclosure of AI evaluation processes and outcomes. This transparency helps to build public trust and confidence in the technologies being developed.

Secondly, collaboration fosters innovation and continuous improvement. Regulatory bodies can provide valuable insights and feedback to AI developers, helping to identify potential risks and areas for improvement. This iterative process ensures that AI systems are continually refined and enhanced, leading to safer and more effective technologies.

Thirdly, a collaborative approach can help to harmonize global AI standards. As countries and organizations observe and learn from the OpenAI-US government partnership, they can adopt similar frameworks and guidelines, promoting a more unified approach to AI governance worldwide. This harmonization can facilitate international cooperation and reduce regulatory fragmentation, making it easier for AI technologies to be developed and deployed responsibly across different regions.

In summary, the collaboration between OpenAI and the US government on GPT-5 is setting important precedents for the future of AI governance. By emphasizing the role of private companies in shaping public policy and demonstrating the importance of a collaborative approach between AI developers and regulatory bodies, this partnership is paving the way for a new era of responsible AI development. The potential influence on future AI governance models is profound, highlighting the need for safety, ethical considerations, and robust regulatory frameworks. Through collaboration, transparency, and continuous improvement, the global community can navigate the challenges of advanced AI technologies and ensure that their benefits are realized in a way that serves the interests of all humanity.

Conclusion

The collaboration between OpenAI and the US government on GPT-5 marks a pivotal moment in the evolution of artificial intelligence, setting a new standard for AI development and governance. This book has explored the various facets of this partnership, highlighting its significance, objectives, and the broader implications for the future of AI.

Throughout the chapters, we delved into the background of OpenAI's AI models, tracing the evolution from GPT-1 to GPT-4 and anticipating the transformative capabilities of GPT-5. The groundbreaking nature of this partnership was emphasized, with a focus on safety and ethical considerations, and the critical role of the US AI Safety Institute in setting guidelines for AI measurement and policy.

We examined the potential impact of GPT-5 across various industries, from healthcare and education to finance and the creative arts. While the advancements promised by GPT-5 are significant, they come with challenges, including concerns about job displacement and the homogenization of creative output. The need for robust ethical guidelines and safeguards to prevent misuse was a recurring theme, underscoring the importance of responsible AI development.

Data privacy emerged as a crucial concern, particularly regarding federal access to GPT-5's inner workings and the need for stringent safeguards to protect user data. Measures for ensuring transparency and accountability were discussed, highlighting the importance of public trust in AI technologies.

The global implications of this partnership were explored, with an emphasis on how it could influence AI development worldwide and the potential for an era of AI nationalism. The collaboration sets a precedent for future AI governance, demonstrating the importance of integrating safety and ethical considerations into AI development.

In setting precedents, this partnership highlights the role of private companies in shaping public policy and the implications for government policy. The collaborative approach between AI developers and regulatory bodies was shown to be essential, fostering innovation, transparency, and continuous improvement.

Looking to the future, the insights gained from this collaboration offer a roadmap for AI governance. As GPT-5 and subsequent models continue to advance, the principles established by this partnership will guide their development, ensuring they are deployed safely and ethically. The potential impact of GPT-5 is vast, promising to revolutionize industries and improve lives, but it must be managed with care and foresight.

As we conclude, it is essential to recognize the ongoing journey of AI development. The collaboration between OpenAI and the US government is just one step in a broader effort to harness the power of AI responsibly. The future of AI governance will depend on continued vigilance, innovation, and cooperation among stakeholders.

To readers, your role in this journey is vital. Staying informed and engaged with AI developments is crucial as these technologies become more integrated into our lives. By understanding the complexities and implications of AI, you can contribute to the dialogue and help shape the future of AI governance.

In conclusion, the story of GPT-5 and its collaboration with the US government is a testament to the potential of AI to drive progress and the necessity of managing it responsibly. As we move forward, let us embrace the opportunities AI presents while remaining mindful of the ethical and societal challenges it brings. Together, we can navigate this new frontier and ensure that AI technologies serve the interests of all humanity.

www.ingramcontent.com/pod-product-compliance
Lightning Source LLC
Chambersburg PA
CBHW071958210526
45479CB00003B/983